Simple Guide to Saving

For the Young & Broke

by Vicki Fitzgerald

Simple Guide to Saving

For the Young & Broke

Illustrated by Katie Lei: www.katieleicreative.com

Dedication

This book is dedicated to my awesome husband Sean who has shared this journey with me for over 30 years, and my daughter Gina & son Brian who continue to astonish me with their frugality.

Contents:

Part 1.
Be Aware of your Spending............ 7

Part 2.
Live Beneath your Means............ 35

Part 3.
Invest the Difference:
Let Time Work for You,
Not Against You.........................67

Acknowledgements

Writing this has been fun, especially since I've gotten lots of help and suggestions! But please note that any mistakes are mine alone.

Several smart, generous people read this booklet and gave me valuable feedback, including Mark Treger (who taught me at a young age that the best thing that money buys is freedom), Randhi Wilson, Mikki McClish, Brenda Eichelberger, Skip Lei (the Simple Guy), Sean Fitzgerald, and my favorite 20-somethings Gina Fitzgerald and Brian Fitzgerald. I am indebted to them!

Thanks also to Katie Lei, the 20-something who created the wonderful illustrations throughout this book. Check out her website at www.katieleicreative.com.

Why Read This?

This doesn't apply to me. I pay my bills and meet expenses (usually). Besides, I'm too broke to save any money. I don't have a problem!

> But the truth is,
>
> - it's OK to be young and broke,
> - **but it sucks** to be old and poor.
>
> Let's prevent that.

That won't happen to me!

Many people my age (mid-50's) fear the future. They barely meet their expenses and lack any hope of retiring. Sadly, it's quite common.

> - The Mean (*average*) retirement savings of families between 50 and 55 is $124,831
> - The Median *(middle value in a list from low to high)* retirement savings of families between 50 and 55 is $8000.

Not enough to live well in retirement.[1]

Being old may seem far away, but it's important to start saving **now**, even with minimal money. **Make time work for you**, not against you.

- Getting your financial life on track and saving money leads to a more contented life.

---

[1] Source: www.cnbc.com, *How much the Average Family Has Saved for Retirement at every age.*

Saving Money? Sounds too Hard

Saving money isn't hard, it's just **intentional**. You don't have to be a budget freak or a Wall Street guru.

You just need to:
1. be aware of your spending,
2. live beneath your means (income),
3. then invest the difference to let time work for you, not against you.

We discuss how.

Why Listen to Me?

First off, I'm no financial wizard. Plus, I'm way older than you. But I do speak from experience:

- Working class girl, two sisters, single mom who supported us on a secretary's salary.
- Having little money taught me a ton.
- Paid for college and grad school through work (2-3 part-time jobs in college, full-time job during MBA School), scholarships, modest loans, and by being extremely frugal.
- I've stumbled. After quitting my first real job I got my 401k retirement plan payout and spent every penny. It was fun...until the IRS letter came - a big fat tax bill with penalties. Ouch!
- Now live financially independently and debt-free in the Pacific Northwest. My husband and I work when we want and enjoy free time and frequent travel.

> *To us, freedom is having the means to do what we want!*

I admit that it's been many years since I've faced the **tremendous** challenges of being young and broke. But I hope that you can learn something from my struggles.

Here's how we did it. Starting in our 20s, we followed the three steps outlined in this booklet:

1. We were very **aware** of our spending (to the point of being a little obsessive)
2. We always lived **beneath** our means (spent less than we made)
3. We **invested the difference**, which allowed **time** to work for us, not against us.

It can work for you too. Let's get started!

P.S. I'm friends with Skip Lei who wrote *The Simple Guy Diet* booklet. I modeled this simple booklet after his. He said it was OK.

Part 1. Be Aware of your Spending

Part 1. Be Aware of your Spending

Awareness is knowing:

> ## How much money you waste:
> *What you spend on non-essential items.*
>
> ## The opportunity cost of that money:
> *How much that wasted money would be worth over time.*

How much do you waste?

Meet Ashley, 25. On a typical Friday she spends this.

Item	Cost
Mocha & muffin	$ 8
Lunch at work cafeteria	$ 7
After work drinks	$15
Uber home (instead of bus)	$13
Total spending for the day	**$43**

$43 isn't much, right? Let's add it up to see a typical week:

Non Essential spending multiplied by...	Days /Wk =	Total Spent in 1 Week
Mocha & Muffin: $8	5	$ 40
Lunch at work cafeteria: $7	5	$ 35
Friday drinks: $15	1	$ 15
Friday Uber home (instead of bus): $13	1	$ 13
Quick dinner out or carry out: $12	2	$ 24
Saturday dinner and drinks out: $23	1	$ 23
Total Spending for the Week		**$150**

There are many cheaper alternatives.

Spending on
non-essentials
equals Wasted Money!

In one year, Ashley's weekly wasted spending ($150) is a whopping $7800!

Wasted Money *that she could have saved* in just one years time:
$7800!

Opportunity Cost of that Money

How much would that wasted money be worth over time (opportunity cost)?

- **$1.00 invested (not wasted) at age 25 will likely be worth $10.00 before age 45, and will gain $.50 per year from age 45 on, forever.**

There are many books and articles on how to do this. It's easy and will be explained in Part 3.

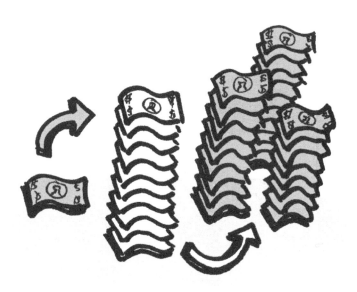

So had Ashley invested just *one weeks worth of wasted money*:

- $150 invested at age 25 will likely be worth $1500 before age 45.

- Then had she invested **a years worth** of wasted money, in 20 years:

$7800 invested at age 25 will likely be worth **$78,000** before age 45.

Instead of wasting that hard earned cash, let it work for **you**!

To Do: Commit to a 40 Day Plan

Here's a simple plan to allow you to become **aware of your spending**. But it takes time.

Psychologists like 40 days, in that if you want to change, it takes about that long to form a new habit. It's kind of magical.

- If you work/study during the week, it's best to start on a Saturday or Sunday.

Note you aren't changing forever, just committing to 40 days to become aware of your spending. And it gets easier and more empowering each day!

Get a Notebook & Record all of your Spending

OK, I can be a little obsessive. But this worked for me.

Buy a cheap, one-subject spiral bound notebook, in a color you like if possible. This is your first step toward clarity, honesty, and transparency.

If you are diligent about recording your spending on your phone, do that each day, but at the end of each day, re-record in your notebook.

Leave the first page of your notebook blank (for income to be recorded later).

Then draw four columns with the following headings at the top of the next page:

1. Take a deep breath!
2. Let's tackle your regular bills first. Enter the **first three columns (Date/Cost, Item, Want or Need?)** for **every** recurring expense that you have for the month, this may include (but not limited to) rent, utilities, car, insurance, phone, etc.

It takes time to gather, but **it's worth it**.

Whew! Pat yourself on the back for doing such a good job!

After Recording your Regular Monthly Expenses....

3. **Each day** record *everything you spend for one week*. Complete the first three columns for each item.

   Carry your notebook everywhere, or carry a piece of paper, or use your phone to record each purchase and then complete the first three columns in your notebook when you get home.

Notes

Good job recording your spending for a week!

- Now go to page one of your notebook and record your previous month's **income**.

- Then return to the top of your spending list and complete the **fourth column** for your previous week's spending. Repeat each day.

  Really think about whether your spending was **worth it** after one weeks' time. Do any patterns appear? Habits? Ordering food in when you are tired?

Notes

OK, you're in! Now think **before** spending!

- *The trick is to be aware of what we waste and gradually stop wasting!*

Continue completing the first three columns each day you spend. Complete the fourth column for the previous week's spending asking, "Were those purchases really needed?"

Notes

After week four, return to page one and record your income for the previous four weeks (month 2). Then continue recording your spending.

- *Are you becoming more aware of your spending?*

Being aware of your spending
leads to less wasted money.

Notes

I'd hate myself if I didn't warn you. Using credit cards can lead to wasting and spending what you don't have.

> If you don't pay your credit card balances **in full every month,** you pay WAY too much in interest – you're being ripped off.

Let's see what Ashley did:[2]

- Over time, she charged $5000.
- She pays the minimum payment of $200 each month.

Ashley's Credit Card Balance	$5000
Credit Card Interest Rate	18.9%
Minimum Payment Percentage	4%
Ashley's monthly (minimum) payment	$ 200

If she makes *no other purchases on the card* and only *pays the minimum,* it will take her:

- **11 years and 5 months** to pay off the $5000 debt
- & the total she will have to pay is **$8109.16**

Grim, isn't it?

---

[2] Try it: Go to interest.com, Calculators/Credit Card Calculators/Minimum Payment Calculator

So during this 40 day period (and *forever* unless you pay your full balance each month), STOP using credit cards. Use cash, write a check, or use a debit card.

- It got easier over time.

- I eliminated the anxiety of asking myself, "where did all my money go?"

- Judging whether the spending was worth it at different times made me more discriminating of my spending.

- I saw exactly how much money I wasted and acknowledged that I needed to stop.

Part 2. Live Beneath your Means

Part 2. Live Beneath your Means

You're on your way! Now do the math. Total your income and your spending for the same time periods. If your income = expenses or is less than your expenses, then you are **not** living beneath your means.

> Income > Spending – Good!
> Income = Spending – Not the worst, but still Bad!
> Income < Spending – Bad!

Income exceeds your spending? Congrats! You're living beneath your means, but you can still benefit from this booklet by cutting wasted spending and investing any extra.

In Big Trouble?

Deep in debt? You probably need more than this simple method. Go to: *https://www.usa.gov/debt*. Check out personal finance books from your library. Suze Orman and Dave Ramsey are a couple good authors.

But for many, we just need help on how to stop wasting. That's next.

First, be aware of the spending mindset:

- Recognize the difference between wanting and needing (Grande Frappuccino vs. a home-made coffee).

- The **desire** to have is often more powerful than the pleasure of having it. Marketers know this!
  - Want something? Wait three days before buying.

- The helpful salesperson/ agent/ telemarketer is **not** your friend. They **want your money**!

- *Ego is your opinion of yourself.* I once thought that possessions, like my car or house, determined my and other's opinion of me. I've tamed my ego.

- Ego leads to **comparing** yourself with others based on possessions. We worry that people have better stuff than we have. Truth is, there will **always** be people with more money and possessions than we have.[3]

---

[3] For more on this subject, read Rachel Cruze's book, *Love Your Life Not Theirs.*

Comparison is the thief of joy.

Theodore Roosevelt

Simple things to try:

- *Downsize your order*: instead of a costly, calorie-laden coffee drink, order a simple coffee or tea.

- *Be Patient*: Wait three days before buying. Still need it? Get it. If not, count that as a win!

- *Munch*: Always carry a simple snack with you, like almonds. You won't be tempted to order the lemon pound cake with your coffee, or hit the vending machine when you're not hungry.

- *Employ Public Exposure*: My son and his girlfriend write every purchase and post it on their fridge. It reduces their spending.

- *Borrow*: Use your public library! My library offers the following to borrow for free:
  - 20,000+ e-books & audio titles via an app
  - Games (PS2, Wii, etc.), DVDs
  - Books (regular, audio, graphic novels, non-English, reference books) for fun and on every subject, including personal finance
  - Wi-Fi, P.C.s, Magazines, Tax Instructions
  - Knowledgeable people to help you.

Ya gotta eat, right? Here are some tips on saving money on food/drink.

Drink **water** (not bottled). Order it instead of soda when dining out. Don't keep soda pop, energy drinks, or juice at home.

Prepare your own food. No need to be a chef! Search for simple recipes (mmm... easy black bean soup recipe). Leftovers rule!

Grocery store strategies:

- *Make a list and stick to it.*
- Ban impulse purchases! Stores put pricy items at eye level, offer samples, have candy and other 'grab it' items near checkout. Beware!
- Plan your week's food based on a few yummy sale items.
- NEVER go to the grocery store when you're hungry.
- Only use coupons for things you need and use.
- Shop less in the middle of the grocery store, where the chips, sodas, and expensive premade foods are. Meander the outer edges where the fresh stuff is.

Bring your lunch!

- When working on site, I **pack my lunch**. A lunch box with cold pack is great for leftovers, yogurt, fruit, cheese, nuts.
- I enjoy my own food all day, which keeps me away from the evil vending machine.
- Why? The work cafeterias (and restaurants) are costly and sometimes the food is only so-so.

Dining out strategies:

- *I always drink plenty of water with my meal.* No soda or any pricy beverage.
- Dine at lunch instead of dinnertime. Food is often cheaper.
- Try two appetizers or a soup/small salad instead of an appetizer and a big entrée.
- If possible, eat during happy hour. Same quality food, often smaller portions (bonus! Get two).
- Like fast food occasionally? Check the value menu.
- *The SimpleGuy Diet* booklet suggests having a small snack before going out to eat so you're not starving when ordering.

Reverse Engineer your Favorite Packaged Foods

Like pre-packaged trail mix, quick flavored oatmeal, stuff like that? It's expensive! I make my own trail mix, it's yummy. Here's how:

1. After enjoying your food, save the wrapper for the ingredient list.
2. Visit a store's bulk foods section.
3. Buy the ingredients, estimate quantities based on the order the ingredients appear on the wrapper.
4. At home mix and taste. Good? You've got your recipe!
5. Store the mix and take as needed. I keep mine in the freezer to keep it fresh longer.
6. Or divide the food into small containers/bags to grab and go! It's easy and saves money and waste.

Housing

In my 20s I shared an apartment in Chicago with two strangers. My room was unheated – brrrrr, and we couldn't have a microwave because of crappy old electrical wiring and fuses. But it was WAY cheap, and near the train station! I loved it!

Where do you live? How much is it: rent/mortgage; insurance; upkeep; maintenance; etc.?

Ponder:

- How much space do you really need?
- Is it feasible to move to a smaller/less expensive place?
- Should you get a roommate/border?
- Can you rent a room somewhere?

Cheaper options are often available depending on your location. Evaluate your living situation often.

49

How do you get around? Consider:

- Expensive car? Is it tied to your ego?
- Can you manage without a car? Research public transportation options.
    - The average cost to own a car is **$706/month** (depreciation, maintenance/repair, and fuel[4]).
- Have a car?
    - Perform regular maintenance! Change the oil/inspect. This avoids future costly repairs.
    - Compare car insurance companies/rates often, even in the middle of a policy period – it's OK to switch.
- Instead of ride sharing, see if public transportation goes to areas you frequent. The few extra minutes of commute time will save dramatic amounts.

---

[4] Source: American Automobile Association: newsroom.aaa.com/auto/your-driving-costs based on 15,000 miles driven annually, August 2017.

Need wheels?

- Consider a **used** car. New cars depreciate (lose value) immediately. Have an unbiased mechanic inspect it first.
- Reconsider purchasing an expensive large vehicle (truck, van, SUV):
  - Only need that extra space 5% of the time?
  - Rent/borrow a truck/van when needed, or pay for delivery.
  - Instead, purchase a vehicle for your day-to-day needs, likely smaller, cheaper, and more energy efficient.

Have kids? They're great, but expensive! Try this:

- For clothes, equipment, and toys, shop resale and garage sales; ask friends and family for hand-me-downs, host a toy/clothing swap.
    - Bonus: Recycling = no packaging.

- Ponder before enrolling your child in (often expensive) activities. Be aware that "Club" or "Elite" sports can be very pricy, time consuming, and fraught with added expenses (like travel).
    - Let your kids be bored sometimes. It promotes imagination and creativity!

- Frequently evaluate your child care needs. Can you share resources with another family? Swap babysitting?

Note that the blocks spell savings!

The fashion industry wants your money every season. Beware!

First, shop your own closet. I love Sara Dalquist[5] who suggests that your clothes follow the five "f's"

- fit, flatter, function, feel good, and friendly (works well with the rest of your wardrobe). Consider these five "f's" before purchasing anything.

Also:

- Don't buy anything just because it's on sale.
- Buy it used from resale stores.
- Host a clothing swap with friends.
- Sell it! Check consignment stores to consign/sell your unneeded items.
- Special occasion? Can you borrow/rent clothes? Or try resale stores.
  - My daughter bought her prom dress at Goodwill. The beautiful gown had the retail tags intact (originally $400). She paid $12!
  - Fast forward: she chose her fabulous wedding gown at a bridal resale shop. She looked gorgeous on her day.

---

[5] Sara Dahlquist, personal stylist, writes for the *Oregonian* and elsewhere. Find her at www.dahlstyle.com

We gotta stay fit. I use my gym often, so it's worth it.

- Have a gym membership?
  - Using it? Stopped going after the first couple months? If so, quit and save the monthly fee.
  - Can you join a cheaper club?
- Before joining a gym, look for *no contract deals*. Then if you're not going, you can quit without penalties.
- Investigate community and other recreation centers that offer low-cost classes, weights, pools, etc.

- Explore **free** ways to stay fit like walking, hiking, running, home exercising, etc.

Married to your cell plan? Can you ditch it?

- Evaluate your needs frequently. Is your plan over-stuffed?
- Consider a "non-smart" phone to save a bundle.
- Really need the latest phone? Look online for refurbished models.
- Can you find a cheaper plan? Research phone plans outside of the major carriers.
- Streaming everything on your phone? Use secure Wi-Fi networks when available, and download music, books, or your local Google Maps area to reduce streaming costs.
- Need your land line? Unless your home doesn't have cell coverage, the answer is probably no.

We pay for content that we really don't need.

- Think about cutting cable TV.
- Be patient.
  - No need to watch it right on release date.
  - Look for the tons of free content out there.

- Like seeing a movie in a theatre occasionally? Me too!
  - Attend a matinee.
  - Does your theatre have discount days?
  - Enjoy cheaper theatres offering second run movies.

- Recognize that shopping is **not** entertainment!

I buy my favorite products when on sale and use coupons.

Buy cheaper **store brands** for lotions, shampoos, soaps, cotton balls, bandages, etc. Medicines too – just check the active ingredients vs. the name brand.

Hair/Nail strategies:

- Feel you must frequent an expensive salon? Shop around! Reasonably priced skilled hairdressers abound. It's OK to break up with your hairdresser!
- Color your hair? DIY or have a friend help. Just follow the directions.
- Go to beauty school and have your hair done by a supervised student.
- Manicure your own nails for a fraction of the cost. It's simple!

Before buying something big (e.g., computer, car, appliance, power tool, vacuum cleaner, etc.) consider:

- Can you borrow, rent, or buy it used?
- If not, research and compare.

Best Research Tool Ever: *Consumer Reports*[6] magazine

I use it to research every major purchase. It's unbiased, tests and rates almost everything, includes general pricing, and highlights good buys. Most libraries carry it, so check it out.

After researching and determining what you need, then search the internet for the best price. Happy hunting!

---

[6] *Consumer Reports* has been independently testing products since 1936, over 7000 products are rated in their labs, they have no outside advertising, and never accept free samples.

- felt in control of my spending.

- stopped worrying if I'd be able to pay my bills each month.

- stopped shopping just because I was bored.

- found joy when I didn't spend for long periods of time.

- challenged myself to get the best value for my dollar and enjoyed it!

- became more grateful for what I have, and not upset about what I don't have.

You are:

- leaving a "smaller footprint." Buying less and buying used items contributes to a world with less packaging, fuel costs, and garbage!

- living more consciously. You're considering the impact your spending has on yourself, your loved ones, and the planet.

- making healthier financial decisions leading to a more contented life.

- becoming more frugal with your time.

- fully realizing that possessions don't define you.

Part 3. Invest the Difference: Let Time Work for You, not Against You

Part 3. Invest the Difference: Let Time Work for You, Not Against You

Congratulations on recording your spending and cutting your wasted spending!

Once you live below your means, you can **save and invest** some of that hard earned cash.

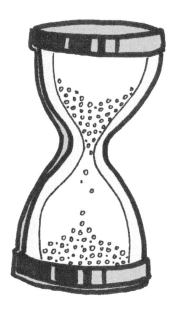

Disclaimer: Please note that the information in this book is not meant as specific investment advice, since any advice of that sort would need to take into account such things as each reader's willingness and need to take risk.

There are a million options for saving and investing. I'll stick to the basics.

First things first:

- Carrying expensive credit card debt? Pay that off **first** (refer to the PSA on p. 31).

- Save up roughly 3-6 months worth of living expenses in cash (or short-term savings) for emergencies.

- *PLAN to save money*. Pay yourself first on payday. Try to save 10-15% of your income. If possible, make your savings contribution automatic.

- If you don't understand it, don't invest in it.

- If your employer offers a 401k retirement plan, it's so smart to *contribute as much as you can* (bonus! it's pre-tax money), especially if they match funds. Contributing when you're in your 20's lets time work for you!

Now watch Ashley **make her money work for her** over time.

I used historic return rates as a basis for Ashley's scenario.[7] While past performance is never a guarantee of future results, you have to make some assumptions.

HISTORIC RETURN RATES 1926-2015	
INFLATION	2.9%
US TREASURY BILLS	3.4%
5-YEAR FIXED TERM INVESTMENTS	5.0%
LONG-TERM GOVERNMENT BONDS	5.6%
US LARGE-COMPANY STOCKS	10.0%
US SMALL-COMPANY STOCKS	12.0%

---

[7] As shown above, the source of these metrics is Ibbortson SBBI 1926-2015. I used this to plug in an assumed 8% return rate in the Time Value of Money Calculator next. There's no guarantee of course, but I figured it was a bit lower than the historic U.S. Stock gains.

Next I entered Ashley's info/assumptions into a *Time Value of Money Calculator*[8]

Annual savings amount (what she saves by not wasting)	$7800
Annual increase in contributions - assume she increases her savings each year by 10%, e.g., *Year 2 she saves $8580:* $7800+(10% of $7800 which is $780) Then each year she increases her amount saved by 10%	10%
Number of years for this analysis (she will be 45)	20
Assume: Before-tax return on savings (see footnote #7).	8%
Assume: Marginal tax bracket	25%

---

[8] Source: financialengines.com education center. Try it yourself using your own numbers.

Based on Ashley's savings schedule, she will accumulate **$727,659 by the time she is 45!**[9]

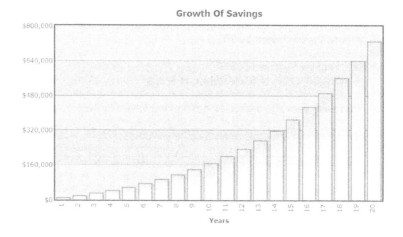

[9] Source: financialengines.com education center. Results based on the assumptions previously entered for Ashley.

Go Ashley!

On the other hand, in 2017 the estimated median savings for a U.S. 40-something was only $63,000. Too small on the path to a healthy retirement.[10]

Now we turn to investing.

---

[10] Source:Investopedia

First a few definitions:

Stock: A share of a company held by an individual or group. Corporations raise money by issuing stock. When you buy stock, you own a piece of the corporation's assets and earnings.

Market Capitalization: The market size of the company. Calculation: (number of shares outstanding) x (the share price of the company's stock). A *large-cap* company has a market capitalization over $10 billion. A *small-cap* company has less than $2 billion, and a *mid-cap* company has between $2 and $10 billion.

Equity: Ownership interest in a firm. This word is sometimes used interchangeably with stock market investments.

Bond: A debt issued for a period of more than one year. Sold by governments, districts, companies, others. When you (the investor) buy bonds, you lend money to the seller. The seller repays the principal (initial amount) of the loan at a specified time and also pays you interest periodically.

Index fund: An investment fund designed to match the returns on a stock market index. A mutual fund whose portfolio matches that of a broad-based index such as the S & P 500 (the 500 most widely held stocks in the New York Stock Exchange or NASDAQ – large-cap companies) and whose performance therefore mirrors the market as represented by that index.

Portfolio: A collection of investments.

Investing can be complicated or easy. I choose **easy.** I love the book by Allan S. Roth, *How a Second Grader Beats Wall Street.*[11] He argues to keep things simple.

The prevailing wisdom is that the young can tolerate more investment risk over the long term than the old. They have more time to weather any stock market swings and work to make up losses.

---

[11] Allan S. Roth, *How a Second Grader Beats Wall Street*, 2009 still holds up to the test of time. He suggests bonds be invested in a tax defered account.

Mr. Roth suggests this for a simple aggressive risk level:

Portfolio Mix:

US Stocks:	60%
Foreign Stocks:	30%
Bonds:	10%

As an alternative I entered the *following* (appropriate for the young) into The Asset Allocation Mix wizard on the CNN Money website:[12]

- Time horizon: *20+ years*
- Risk tolerance: *High*
- Flexibility (when you need your money): *Some*
- In a selloff (market fluctuations): *You do nothing*

Their suggested portfolio was similar:

Portfolio Mix:

Large-Cap US Stocks:	50%
Small-Cap US Stocks:	20%
Foreign Stocks:	20%
Bonds:	10%

Either mix is appropriate.

Now how to invest in stocks and bonds?

---

[12] Source: money.cnn.com

Portfolio mix, check. Let's go!

I suggest investing in **low cost index funds** for *all of your stock purchases*, not individual stocks, not high cost "sector" funds, not through a financial planner, nothing fancy.

The Joy of Indexing for Long-Term Investing[13]

- *Indexing* is buying a small portion of all of the stock shares in a broad market index, like the S&P 500.[14] The performance generally matches that of the index that it mirrors.
- An *index fund* is a mutual fund constructed to match or track the components of the market index.
    - You own small percentages of many, many stocks (you mogul, you!).
    - Indexing is passive (no frantic buying and selling), so generally Index Funds have *low operating costs*. They also adhere to certain rules or standards.
    - Index funds generally have broad market exposure, thus making them *less risky* than investing in just a few stocks.
- At this time, indexing **outperformed** most actively managed mutual funds.

---

[13] Much of this information was gathered from Investopedia.

[14] The Standard & Poors 500 Index is a US stock market index that tracks the 500 most widely held stocks on the New York Stock Exchange or NASDAQ. These are large-cap companies.

Ready to jump in? I'd open a *discount brokerage firm* account. Discount firms are usually cheaper than full-service firms and you control your investments. It's not hard!

There are many discount brokers like Schwab, Fidelity, Vanguard, TD Ameritrade, etc.

1. Search the internet for index funds. Compare the operating costs/fees of the funds and firms.[15]
2. Open an account via the firm's website. Call them for assistance and questions.
3. Build your porfolio with index funds based on the mix you want, e.g., x% in a large-cap US stock index fund, x% in foreign index fund, etc.
4. Choose to re-invest dividends and gains to make your funds grow.

Consider bond investing in a tax-defered account, discussed next.

---

[15] It's generally cheaper to buy index funds directly from the source or brokerage firm, e.g., Schwab has many large and small cap index funds available to invest in, as do other firms.

What about Tax-Deferred Retirement Accounts?

If you contribute to your employer's retirement (like 401k) plan, you usually don't have a choice of the bank or brokerage firm.

But to open your own IRA (remember after I quit my job I spent my 401k money? I should have opened up a "Rollover IRA" account and invested the money there), you can usually use a discount broker.

If you qualify, you can deduct your contributions to your IRA from your taxes. There are limits and rules, and different types of IRAs, so research before investing. To learn more, search the internet for "IRA basics."

Now that we've discussed long-term saving tools, let's examine saving for short-term needs, e.g., your emergency fund. You'll need a tool that provides *liquidity: easy access to your money*. While these tools don't offer high interest rates, they do offer liquidity.

Short-term savings tools:

- Savings account (online, at a bank or a credit union)
- High-yield savings account (may require a higher balance)
- Money market account (usually available at discount brokerage firms)

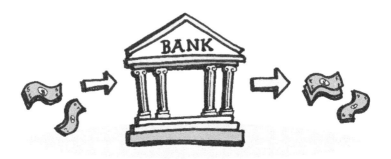

If you invest in simple index funds you don't need one. Why give an advisor a percentage of your hard earned cash?

However, if you're considering hiring a financial advisor/planner, be aware of what's in it for them. Before seeking the advice of a Financial Advisor, you **must** ask:[16]

1. *Are you a fiduciary?* This is an advisor sworn to act in a client's best interest. The answer must be an unequivocal YES.
2. *How do you make money?* Gives you insight into their fees. If they are vague or it takes more than 30 seconds to explain, that's a red flag. Understand the fees.
3. *How do you use technology for my benefit?* They should use tech driven tools in their practice.
4. *How do you help me with taxes?* They should offer advice on optimizing your portfolio for tax purposes.
5. *What other services do you provide to me?* They may provide general 401k advice, etc.

---

[16] Source: CNBC FA Playbook at www.cnbc.com/financial-advisor-playbook/

Occasionally we slip and waste money, or make a very unwise purchase.

The good news (about the bad news) is that you will **be aware of your spending right away.**

What to Do if you Stumble

- If possible, return the item.
- For major purchases, you might be protected by federal and state consumer laws which allow cancellation of certain contracts or sales of goods.
  - The Federal Trade Commission (FTC) requires sellers of goods in certain circumstances to allow consumers a "cooling off" period.
  - This is usually three days in which you can cancel without loss.
- Re-read the tips in this booklet.
- Keep the faith, get right back on track with your notebook and plan!

Being aware of my spending, living beneath my means, and investing the difference resulted in the following. I hope this happens to you! I...

1) am so grateful for what I have. I even use the back of my notebook as a gratitude journal!

2) naturally make better spending choices and am shocked at what people buy.

3) donate items that I no longer require. I don't want unneccesary things.

4) don't compare myself to others unless I'm seeing who can eat the most chocolate.

5) enjoy finding fun things to do that are free.

> Please remember, this book is not a prescription or a guarantee, just something that worked very well for me. Have fun doing this for 40 days and see where it leads you.

I hope by now you realize that saving money isn't hard, it's just intentional.

You just need to

1. be aware of your spending,
2. live beneath your means,
3. then invest the difference to let time work for you, not against you.

It is just this simple! And it gets easier over time.

I wish you all the success in the world!

Have any tips/things that worked for you?
Comments? Share them with me via email at
simplepersonsaves@gmail.com. If there's a next
edition of this book, I may include them!

Websites:[17]

"5 Questions to ask a Financial Planner." *www.cnbc.com/financial-advisor-playbook/.*

"Consumer Issues." *U.S. Government,* www.usa.gov/consumer.

"Credit Card Payoff Calculator." *Interest.com.* www.interest.com/credit-cards/calculators/credit-card-payoff-calculator/

"Dave Ramsey" (links to his books/resources), *Dave Ramsey,* www.daveramsey.com.

"Dealing with Debt." *U.S. Government,* www.usa.gov/debt.

"How much the Average Family Has Saved for Retirement at every age." *www.cnbc.com.*

"Time Value of Money Calculator & Over Time Formula." *Financial Engines Education Center,* financialengines.com/education-center/topics/calculators/time-value-of-money-calculator/.

"Your driving costs based on 15,000 miles driven annually." American Automobile Association. *Newsroom.aaa.com/auto.*

"Suze Orman Financial Solutions for you" (links to her books/resources), *Suze Orman,* www.suzeorman.com.

Books/Articles:

Robin, Vicki, et al. *Your Money or Your Life: 9 Steps to Transforming Your Relationship with Money and Achieving Financial Independence.* Penguin Books, 2008.

Roth, Allan S, *How a Second Grader Beats Wall Street.* John Wiley & Sons, Inc., 2009.

---

[17] Note that URLs may have changed since publication of this book.

Stanley, Thomas J., et al. *The Millionaire Next Door.* Taylor Trade Publishing, 2010.

Sykes, Tanisha A. "Regret over intially not saving enough adds fuel to the fire for marketing exec." *USA Today* August 20, 2017.

About the Author

Vicki Fitzgerald lives with her husband in Portland, OR. With two kids in their 20s out on their own, she saw a need for a simple guide to saving for those just starting out. She earned a B.A. in history from North Park University and an MBA from DePaul University a long time ago and worked in Finance/Accounting for many years.

She's aware that this information is not new or earth shattering, but hopes these simple tools will help.

The author hiking in the Pacific Northwest

Made in the USA
Monee, IL
11 June 2021